AKRON AREA
CATHOLIC AND ORTHODOX CHURCHES

Akron Area CATHOLIC *and* ORTHODOX CHURCHES

A Photographic Pilgrimage

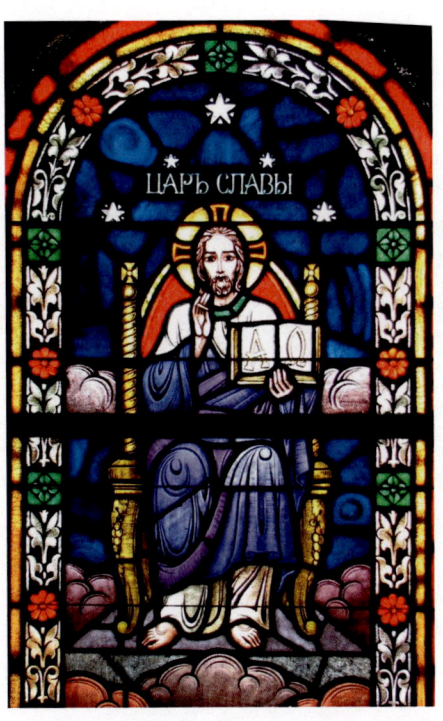

Father Dave Halaiko

Pittsburgh:
Serif Press
2015

Copyright 2015 by Father Dave Halaiko.

Most of the pictures were taken by Father Dave. A few are from Web sites; if there is accidental use of a restricted picture, compensation is available.

Aerial pictures from Bing Maps are reprinted with permission from Microsoft Corporation.

Contents

To the Reader.. 1
Annunciation, Akron, Roman Catholic.. 2
Annunciation, Akron, Greek Orthodox.. 6
Christ the King, Akron, Roman Catholic... 8
Dormition of the Virgin Mary, Akron, Byzantine Catholic............................ 10
Guardian Angels, Copley, Roman Catholic.. 11
Holy Cross Chapel, Akron, at Archbishop Hoban High School................... 12
Holy Family, Stow, Roman Catholic... 13
Holy Ghost, Akron, Ukrainian Byzantine Catholic...................................... 14
Holy Spirit, Uniontown, Roman Catholic.. 17
Holy Trinity, Barberton, Hungarian, Roman Catholic.................................. 18
Immaculate Conception, Akron (Kenmore), Roman Catholic..................... 18
Immaculate Conception, Ravenna, Roman Catholic.................................. 20
Immaculate Heart of Mary, Cuyahoga Falls, Roman Catholic.................... 24
Immaculate Heart of Mary, Kent, Roman Catholic..................................... 26
Infant of Prague Chapel... 27
Loyola Retreat House Chapel.. 28
Mother Most Admirable Chapel, Akron, Roman Catholic........................... 28
Mother of Sorows, Peninsula, Roman Catholic.. 30
Nativity of the Lord Jesus, Akron (Springfield Twp), Roman Catholic........ 31
North American Martyrs Chapel, Walsh Jesuit H. S., Cuyahoga Falls....... 36
Our Lady of the Cedars of Mt. Lebanon, Fairlawn, Maronite Catholic....... 38
Our Lady of the Elms, Akron, Dominican Sisters....................................... 39
Our Lady of the Elms High School, Akron, Dominican Sisters.................. 40
Our Lady of Guadalupe, Macedonia, Roman Catholic............................... 42
Our Lady of Victory, Tallmadge, Romman Catholic.................................... 42
Presentation of Our Lord, Fairlawn, Romanian Orthodox.......................... 44
Prince of Peace, Norton, Roman Catholic... 45
Queen of Heaven, Green, Roman Catholic... 46
Sacred Heart, Akron, Hungarian, Roman Catholic.................................... 48
Sacred Heart, Wadsworth, Roman Catholic.. 49
St. Andrew the Apostle, Norton, Roman Catholic...................................... 50
St. Anne, Rittman, Roman Catholic... 51
St. Anthony, Akron, Italian, Roman Catholic.. 52
St. Archangel Michael, Akron (Springfield Twp), Serbian Orthodox.......... 54

St. Augustine, Barberton, Roman Catholic..56
St. Barnabas, Northfield, Roman Catholic..58
St. Bernard, Akron, Roman Catholic..59
Ss. Cosmas and Damian, Twinsburg, Roman Catholic..64
Ss. Cyril and Methodius, Barberton, Slovak, Roman Catholic....................................65
St. Demetrius, Fairlawn, Serbian Orthodox..68
St. Edward Chapel, Fairlawn, Roman Catholic..70
St. Elia the Prophet, Akron, Macedonian-Bulgarian Orthodox....................................72
St. Eugene, Cuyahoga Falls, Roman Catholic..73
St. Francis de Sales, Akron (Coventry Twp), Roman Catholic....................................74
St. George, Clinton, Roman Catholic...76
St. George, Fairlawn, Antiochean Orthodox...77
St. Hedwig, Akron, Polish, Roman Catholic..78
St. Hilary, Fairlawn, Roman Catholic..79
St. John the Baptist, Akron, Slovak, Roman Catholic...82
St. Joseph, Akron, Melchite Catholic...83
St. Joseph, Cuyahoga Falls, Roman Catholic..84
St. Joseph, Randolph Twp, Roman Catholic..86
St. Martha, Akron, Roman Catholic...90
St. Mary, Akron, Roman Catholic..91
St. Mary, Akron, Orthodox...95
St. Mary, Hudson, Roman Catholic..96
St. Matthew, Akron, Roman Catholic..98
St. Michael, Akron, Byzantine Catholic...99
St. Nicholas, Barberton (Coventry Twp), Byzantine Catholic...................................100
St. Nicholas, Mogadore (Suffield Twp), Russian Orthodox.......................................101
St. Nikola, Green, Macedonian Orthodox..104
St. Patrick, Kent, Roman Catholic..105
St. Paul, Akron (Firestone Park), Roman Catholic..106
St. Peter, Akron (Sherbondy Hill), Roman Catholic..108
St. Peter Claver, Akron, Roman Catholic...109
St. Peter of the Fields, Rootstown, Roman Catholic..110
Ss. Peter and Paul, Doylestown, Roman Catholic..112
Ss. Philip and James, Canal Fulton, Roman Catholic..113
St. Sebastian, Akron, Roman Catholic...114
St. Thomas Hospital Chapel, Akron...116
St. Thomas, Fairlawn, Bulgarian Orthodox..117
St. Victor, Richfield, Roman Catholic...118
St. Vincent de Paul, Akron, Roman Catholic...119

To the Reader

Ohio became a state in 1803. Akron was founded in 1825 on the continental divide. North of the divide, water flows to the Great Lakes; south of the divide, water flows to the Ohio River. Akron (Greek for "high place") is at the summit of the Ohio and Erie Canal, connecting Lake Erie to the Ohio River.

The first Catholics in Akron were Irish canal builders; a church for them was begun in 1837 on Green Street and was named St. Vincent de Paul. The present stone church was built during the Civil War at the top of Market Street hill.

Immigration to Akron began with settlers from Connecticut and from the Atlantic states. The Irish potato famine and civil unrest in Europe led to the arrival of Irish and German immigrants. Akron, like many Ohio towns, needed a second Catholic church for German-speaking people, and St. Bernard Church was established in 1861.

Industry grew rapidly in Akron in the late 19th century, which led to the arrival of immigrants from central, eastern, and southern Europe. Churches were established for them. After World War II, migration to the suburbs began and churches were built in a ring around the city.

The building of expressways, urban renewal, and the loss of the need for ethnic churches, led to the reconfiguration of parishes in the Akron area. Some churches were merged or closed. It is hoped that the pictures in this book will preserve the memory of those churches, and also will show the vibrancy of our present church life.

Catholic and Orthodox churches are a treasury of architecture and art. They are houses of worship and gates of heaven. I have limited this book to pictures of these churches. There are many churches of other religious groups which are beautiful and inspiring, but it will be the task of someone else to record them.

Annunciation, Akron, Roman Catholic

Annunciation, Akron, Roman Catholic

Microsoft product screen shot reprinted with permission from Microsoft Corporation.

Established 1907. Now part of Visitation of Mary Parish.

Annunciation, Akron, Roman Catholic

Annunciation, Akron, Roman Catholic

Annunciation, Akron, Greek Orthodox

Established 1916; church built in 1927; iconography, 1988.

Annunciation, Akron, Greek Orthodox

Christ the King, Akron, Roman Catholic

Established 1935 on Grant Street as a Croatian parish. The church was demolished in 1959 for expressway construction. The parish was moved to northeast Akron and was made a territorial parish. In 2009, it was merged with St. Martha Parish to form Blessed Trinity Parish.

The old church, which stood where the exit ramp from westbound I-76 goes to Grant Street.

Christ the King, Akron, Roman Catholic

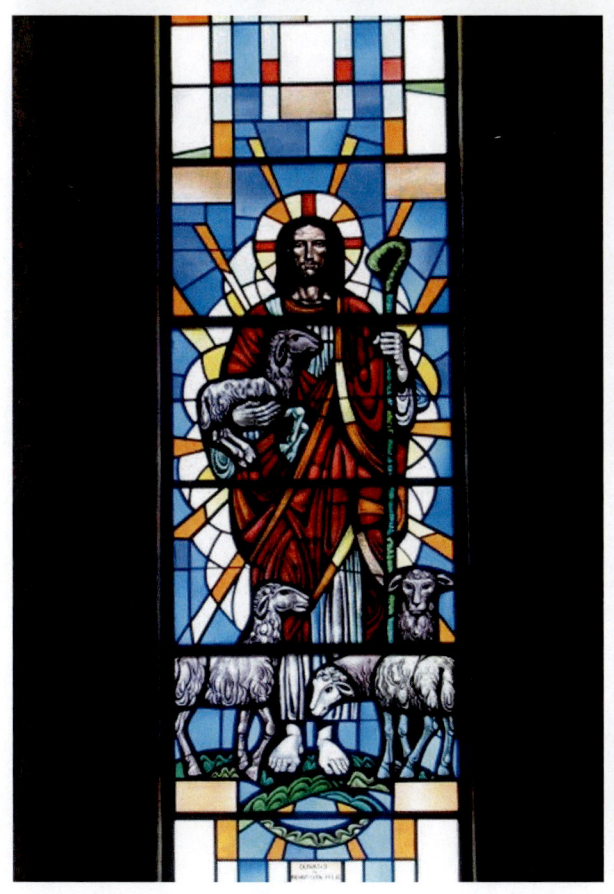

Dormition of the Virgin Mary, Akron, Byzantine Catholic

Established in 1948, it became a Byzantine Catholic parish in 1952. It is now closed.

Guardian Angels, Copley, Roman Catholic

Guardian Angels, Copley, Roman Catholic

Established in 1964.

11

Holy Cross Chapel, Akron

Holy Cross Chapel, Akron, At Archbishop Hoban High School

Part of the Maynard Family Spiritual Center at the school, this chapel was dedicated in 2014.

Holy Family, Stow, Roman Catholic

Holy Family, Stow, Roman Catholic

Established 1946; the church was dedicated January 8, 1961.

13

Holy Ghost, Akron, Ukrainian Byzantine Catholic

Holy Ghost, Akron, Ukrainian Byzantine Catholic

In 1916, the first church (below, right) was built at Washington and Abel Streets. It was torn down for the Grant-Washington Urban Renewal Project. The present church on Brown Street was completed in 1961 and was dedicated on September 3, 1962.

Holy Ghost, Akron, Ukrainian Byzantine Catholic

Holy Spirit, Uniontown, Roman Catholic

Established in 1979.

Holy Trinity, Barberton Hungarian, Roman Catholic

Established in 1911; closed in 2007.

Immaculate Conception, Akron (Kenmore), Roman Catholic

Immaculate Conception, Akron (Kenmore), Roman Catholic

Established in 1923; the present church was built in 1952.

Immaculate Conception, Ravenna, Roman Catholic

Immaculate Conception, Ravenna, Roman Catholic

Established 1841; the present church was dedicated on September 4, 1927.

20

Immaculate Conception, Ravenna, Roman Catholic

Immaculate Conception, Ravenna, Roman Catholic

Immaculate Conception, Ravenna, Roman Catholic

Immaculate Heart of Mary, Cuyahoga Falls, Roman Catholic

Established in 1952.

Immaculate Heart of Mary, Cuyahoga Falls, Roman Catholic

Immaculate Heart of Mary, Kent, Roman Catholic

The church was dedicated on May 13, 1962 and serves as the student parish at Kent State University.

Infant of Prague Chapel

Infant of Prague Chapel

The Carmelites came to Akron in 1947, and this was their chapel. The property is now used by Interval Brotherhood Home.

Loyola Retreat House Chapel

Dedicated June 20, 1965.

Mother Most Admirable Chapel, Akron, Roman Catholic

Mother Most Admirable Chapel, Akron, Roman Catholic

Built in 1966 for the Daughters of Divine Charity, who arrived in Akron in 1943.

Mother of Sorrows, Peninsula, Roman Catholic

The church was completed in 1882 at the cost of $1800.

Nativity of the Lord Jesus, Akron (Springfield Twp), Roman Catholic

Established July 1, 1977. The church was completed in 1992 at the cost of $1,500,000. Below the altar area, there is a replica of the cave in Bethlehem where Jesus was born. There is also a large collection of crèches from many different lands and cultures.

Nativity of the Lord Jesus, Akron (Springfield Twp), Roman Catholic

Microsoft product screen shot reprinted with permission from Microsoft Corporation.

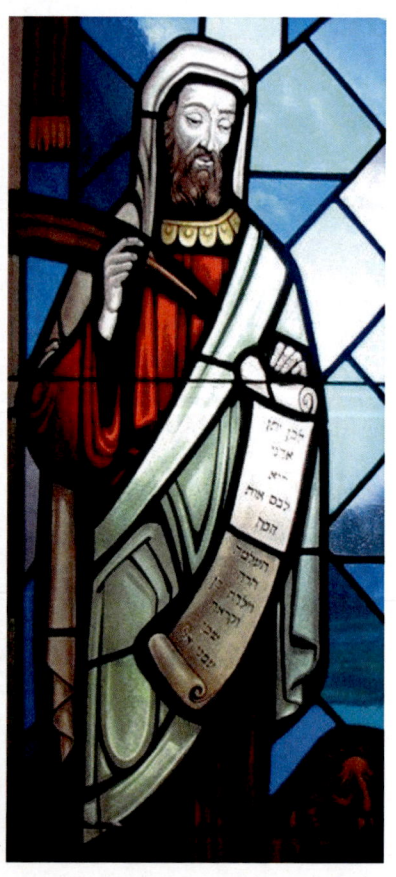

Nativity of the Lord Jesus, Akron (Springfield Twp), Roman Catholic

Nativity of the Lord Jesus, Akron (Springfield Twp), Roman Catholic

Nativity of the Lord Jesus, Akron (Springfield Twp), Roman Catholic

Microsoft product screen shot reprinted with permission from Microsoft Corporation.

There is a wetland behind the church, with a trail around it; along the trail are Stations of the Cross and many types of wildflowers.

North American Martyrs Chapel, Walsh Jesuit H. S., Cuyahoga Falls

North American Martyrs Chapel, Cuyahoga Falls

Our Lady of the Cedars of Mt. Lebanon, Fairlawn, Maronite Catholic

The original church was established 1937 on Codding Street in Akron; it was replaced 1981 with a new church. That building was bought by Akron General Hospital; the parish moved to Fairlawn. Ground was broken April 6, 1985, and the present church was dedicated on October 5, 1986.

Our Lady of the Elms, Akron, Dominican Sisters

Our Lady of the Elms, Akron, Dominican Sisters

The convent was dedicated on October 14, 1923.

Our Lady of the Elms High School, Akron, Dominican Sisters

Our Lady of the Elms High School, Akron, Dominican Sisters

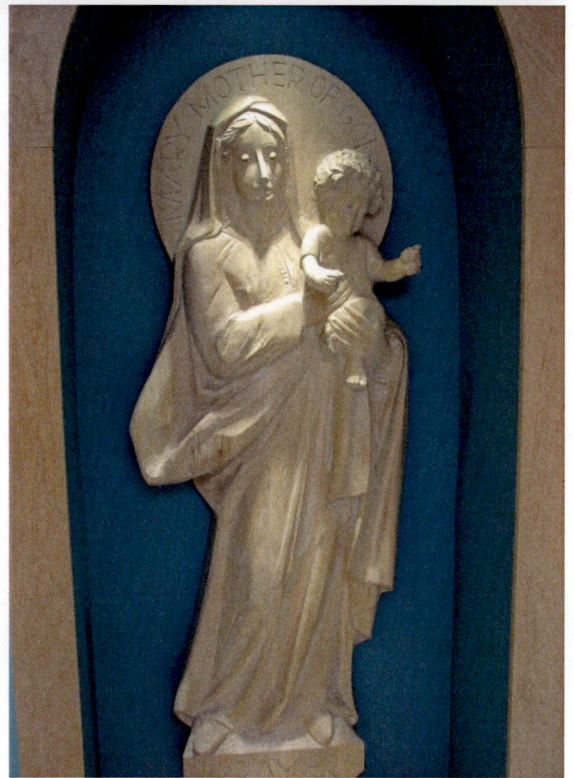

Our Lady of Guadalupe, Macedonia, Roman Catholic

Established in 1967.

Our Lady of Victory, Tallmadge, Roman Catholic

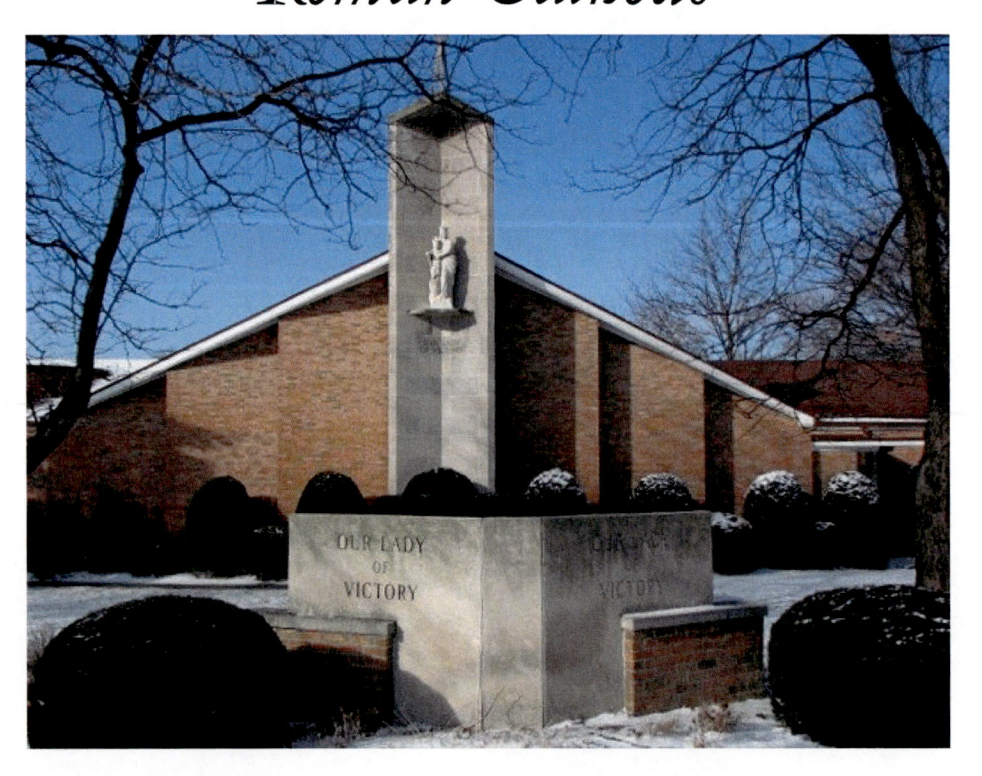

42

Our Lady of Victory, Tallmadge, Roman Catholic

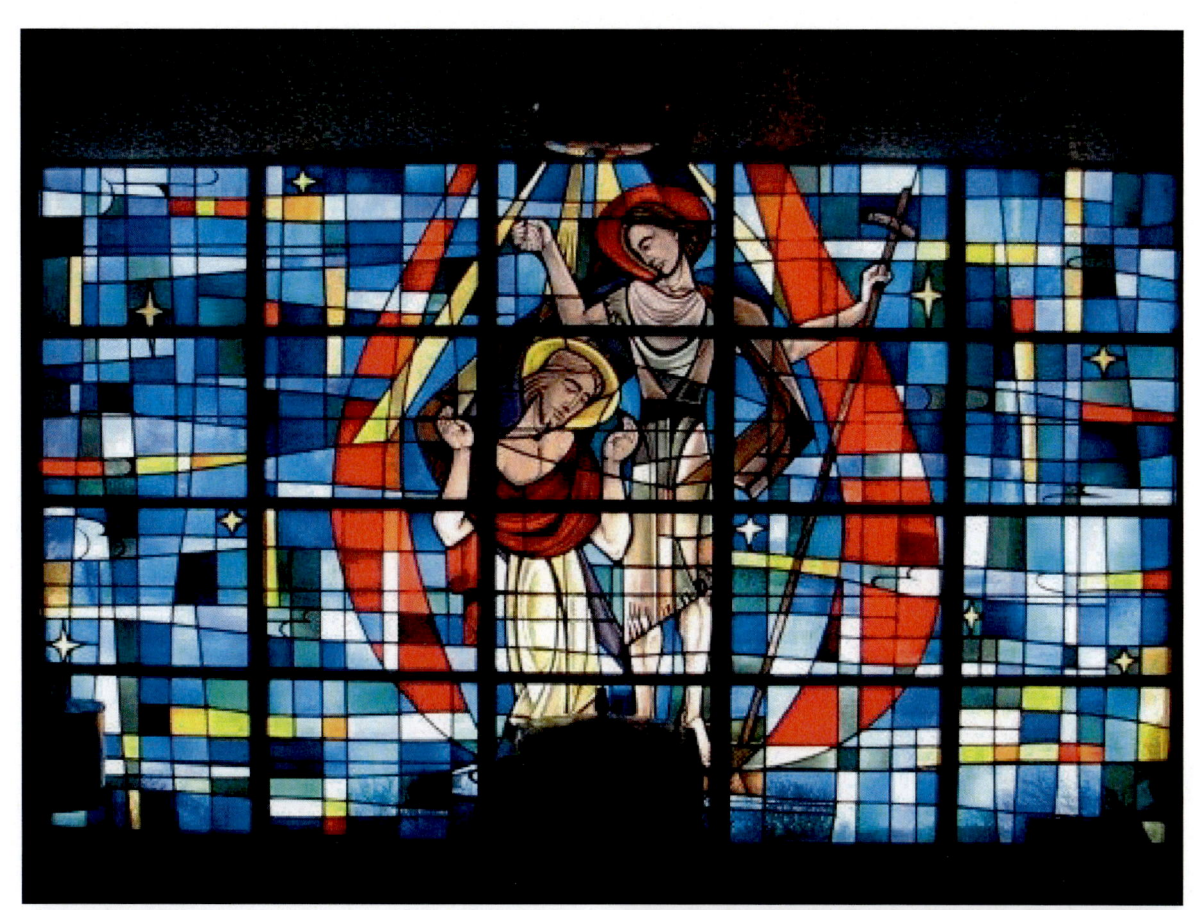

Established in 1944; the present church was dedicated in 1967. The crucifix (right) is from the original church. The window above is in the baptistery.

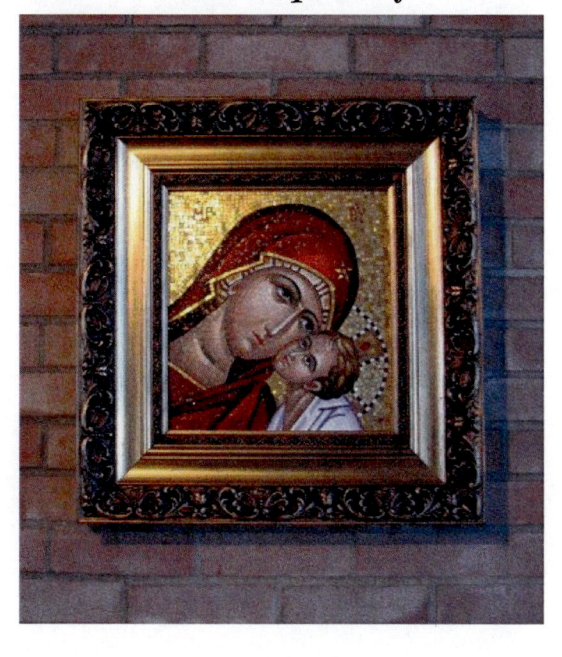

Presentation of Our Lord, Fairlawn, Romanian Orthodox

Presentation of Our Lord, Fairlawn, Romanian Orthodox

Established in 1914; the present church was dedicated in 1967.

Prince of Peace, Norton, Roman Catholic

Prince of Peace, Norton, Roman Catholic

Established in 2002 with the merger of St. Mary and Sacred Heart churches in Barberton. St. Mary was established in 1912 as a Polish parish, and Sacred Heart was established in 1916 as a Slovenian parish. Prince of Peace church was built in 1976 by the parishioners of Sacred Heart.

Old St. Mary, Barberton

Old Sacred Heart, Barberton

45

Queen of Heaven, Green, Roman Catholic

Established
in 1964.

Queen of Heaven, Green, Roman Catholic

Microsoft product screen shot reprinted with permission from Microsoft Corporation.

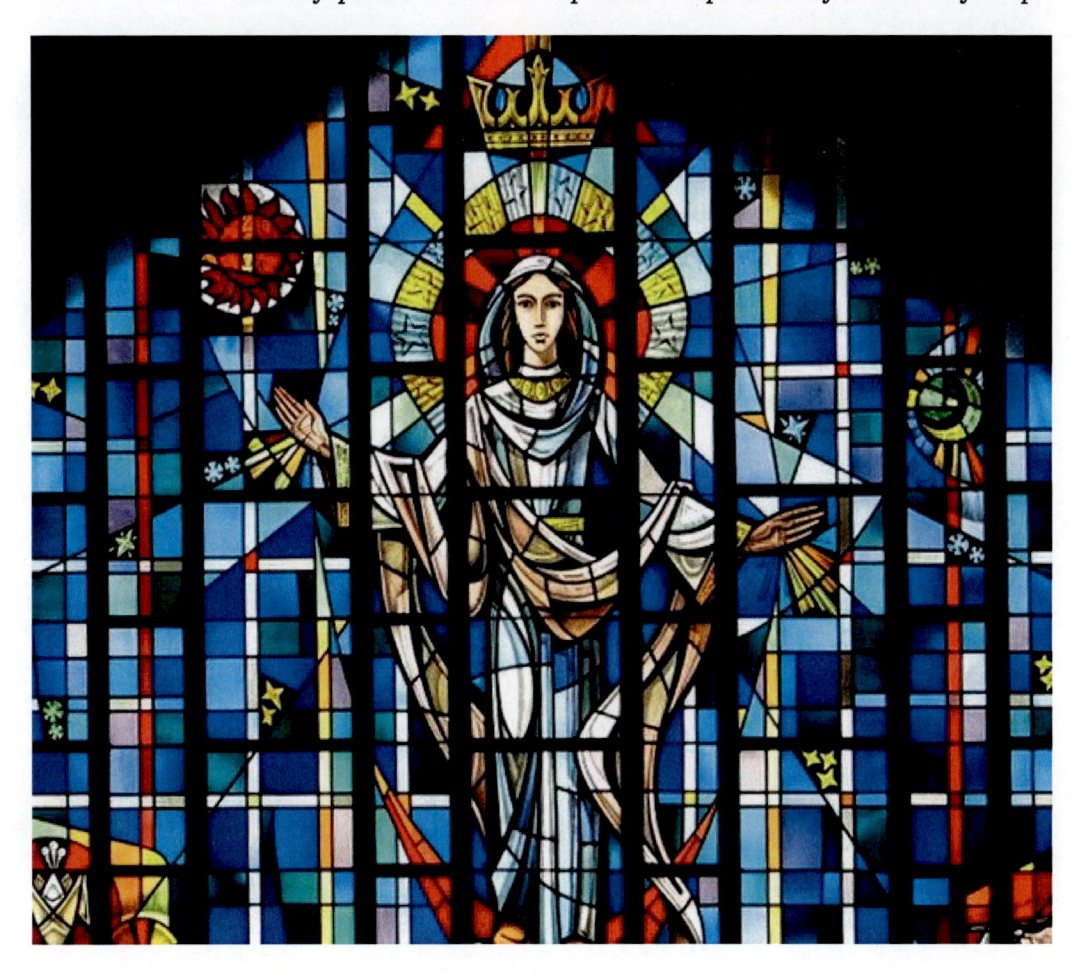

47

Sacred Heart, Akron, Hungarian, Roman Catholic

Established in 1915. The church was dedicated in 1925; the parish was closed in 2010.

Microsoft product screen shot reprinted with permission from Microsoft Corporation.

Sacred Heart, Wadsworth, Roman Catholic

Sacred Heart, Wadsworth, Roman Catholic

Established in 1886; the church was dedicated in 1925.

49

St. Andrew the Apostle, Norton, Roman Catholic

Established in 1951. The church was dedicated on July 26, 1953.

St. Anne, Rittman, Roman Catholic

St. Anne, Rittman, Roman Catholic

Established in 1855.

St. Anthony, Akron, Italian, Roman Catholic

St. Anthony, Akron, Italian, Roman Catholic

Microsoft product screen shot reprinted with permission from Microsoft Corporation.

Established in 1933. The church was completed in 1940; it has excellent stone craftsmanship.

St. Archangel Michael, Akron (Springfield Twp), Serbian Orthodox

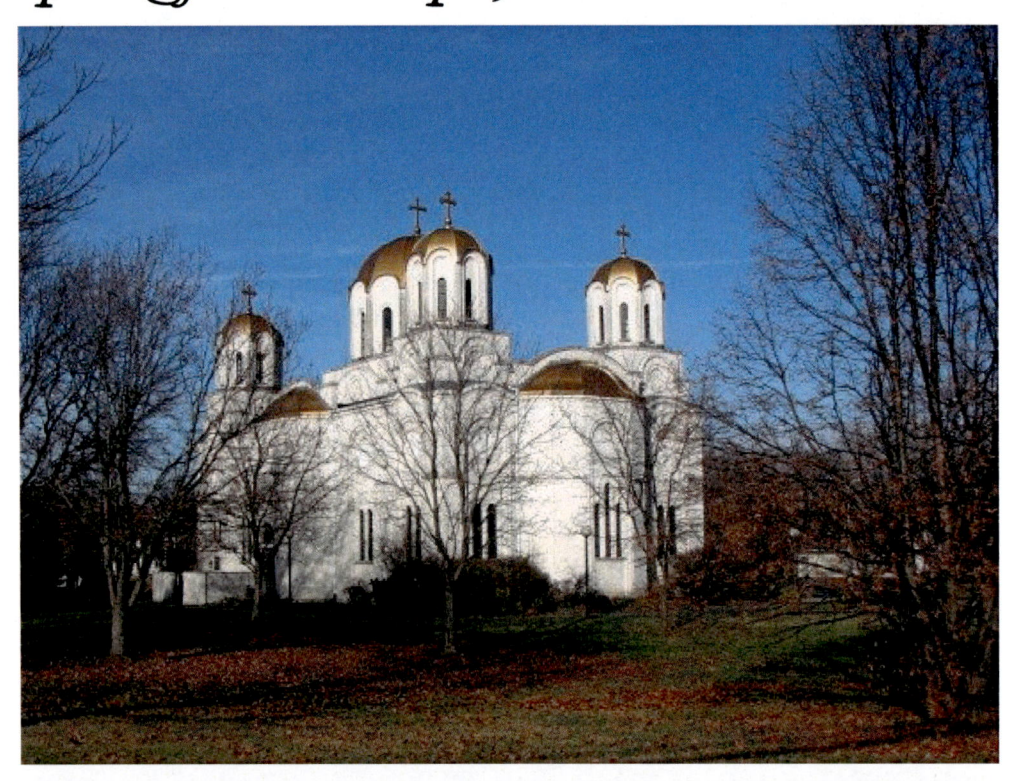

St. Archangel Michael, Akron (Springfield Twp), Serbian Orthodox

The church was built in 1984.

St. Augustine, Barberton, Roman Catholic

St. Augustine, Barberton, Roman Catholic

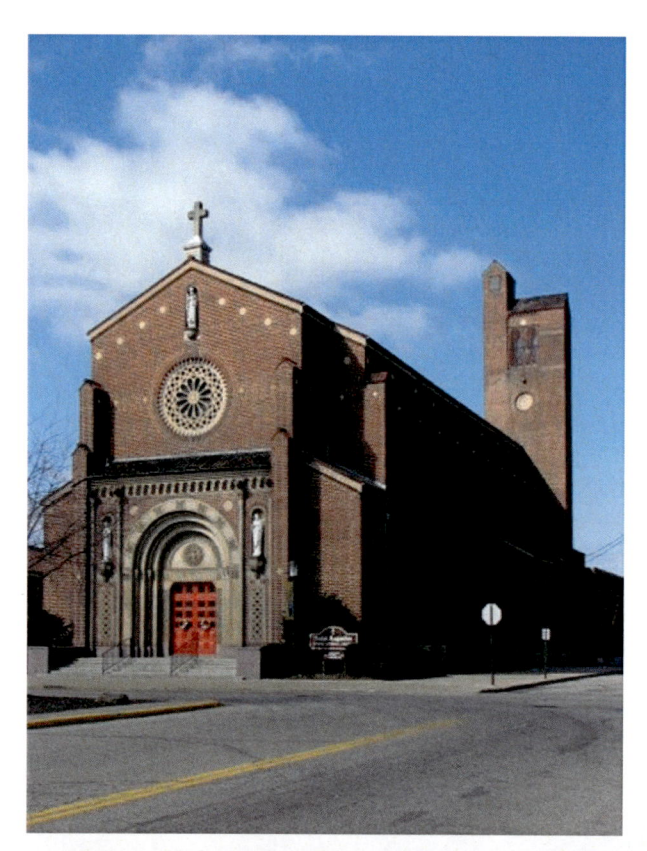

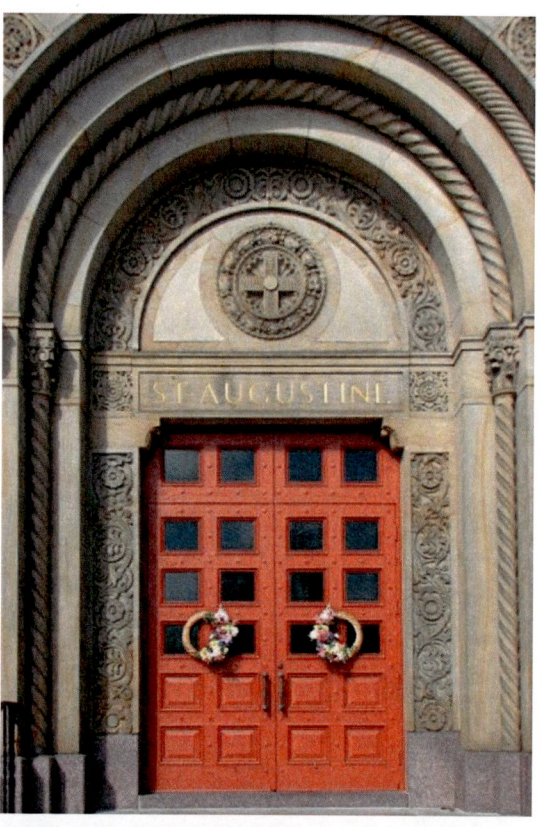

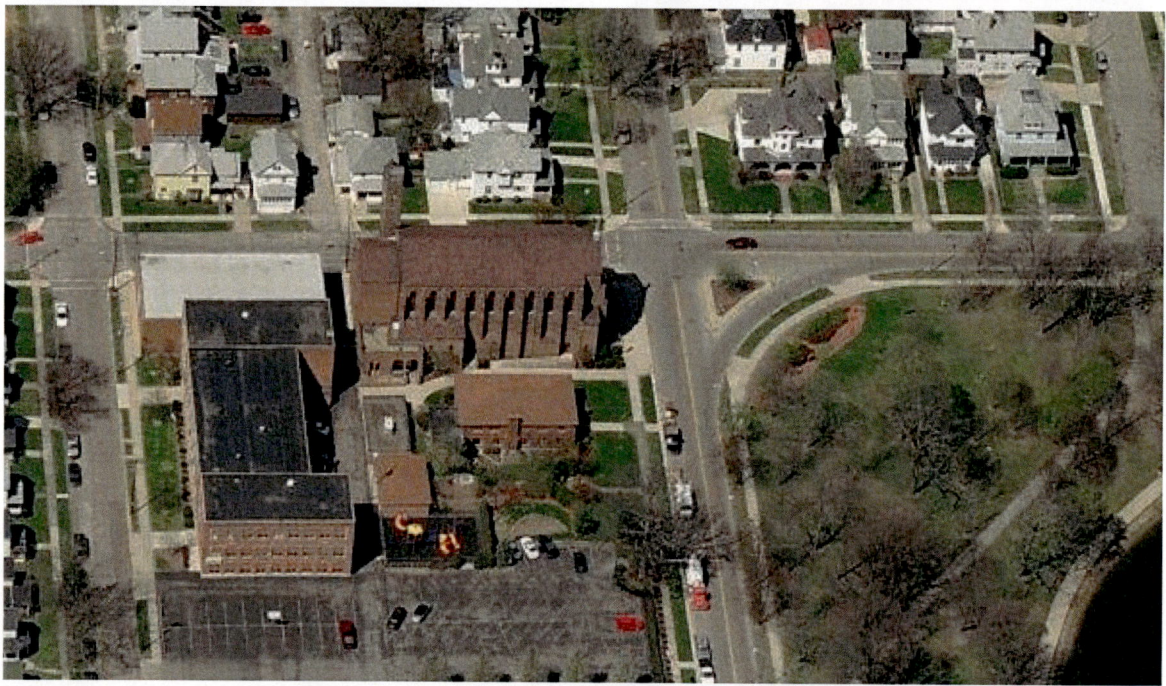

Microsoft product screen shot reprinted with permission from Microsoft Corporation.

St. Augustine, Barberton, Roman Catholic

Established in 1892 as a mission station; it became a parish in 1898. The present church was dedicated on July 5, 1926. St. Augustine is the only area church with a rood cross (below, right).

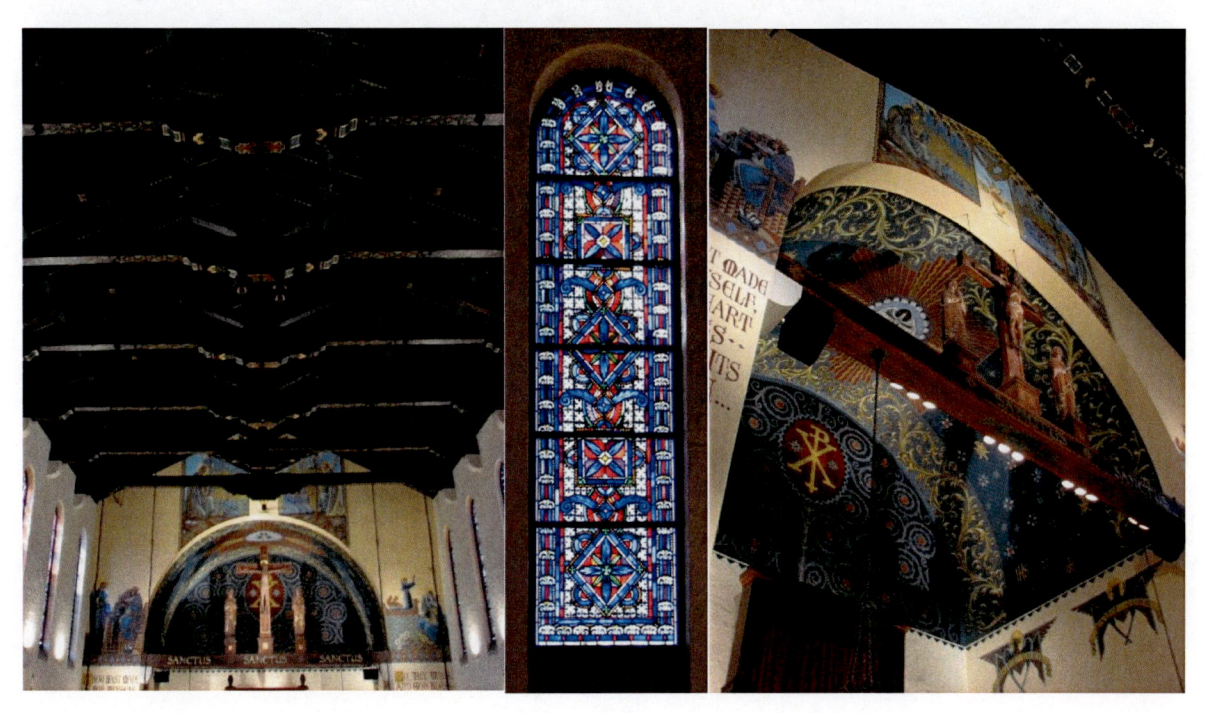

57

St. Barnabas, Northfield, Roman Catholic

Established in 1964.

St. Bernard, Akron, Roman Catholic

Used with the permission of St Bernard Church.

Established in 1861 for German-speaking Catholics.

The first church was on the northeast corner of Broadway and Center Street (now University Avenue). It was brick and cost $5,000. The first Mass there was on June 1, 1863.

The present sandstone church was consecrated on October 15, 1905, and cost $160,000.

In 1908, Slovak and Polish Catholics bought the original brick church and renamed it St. John the Baptist.

St. Bernard Church serves as a metropolitan church, hosting civic events. It is also home to the Hispanic community and to the Newman Campus Ministry of the University of Akron.

St. Bernard, Akron, Roman Catholic

The Summit County Historical Society of Akron, OH; housed at Akron-Summit County Public Library.

The old brick church.

60

St. Bernard, Akron, Roman Catholic

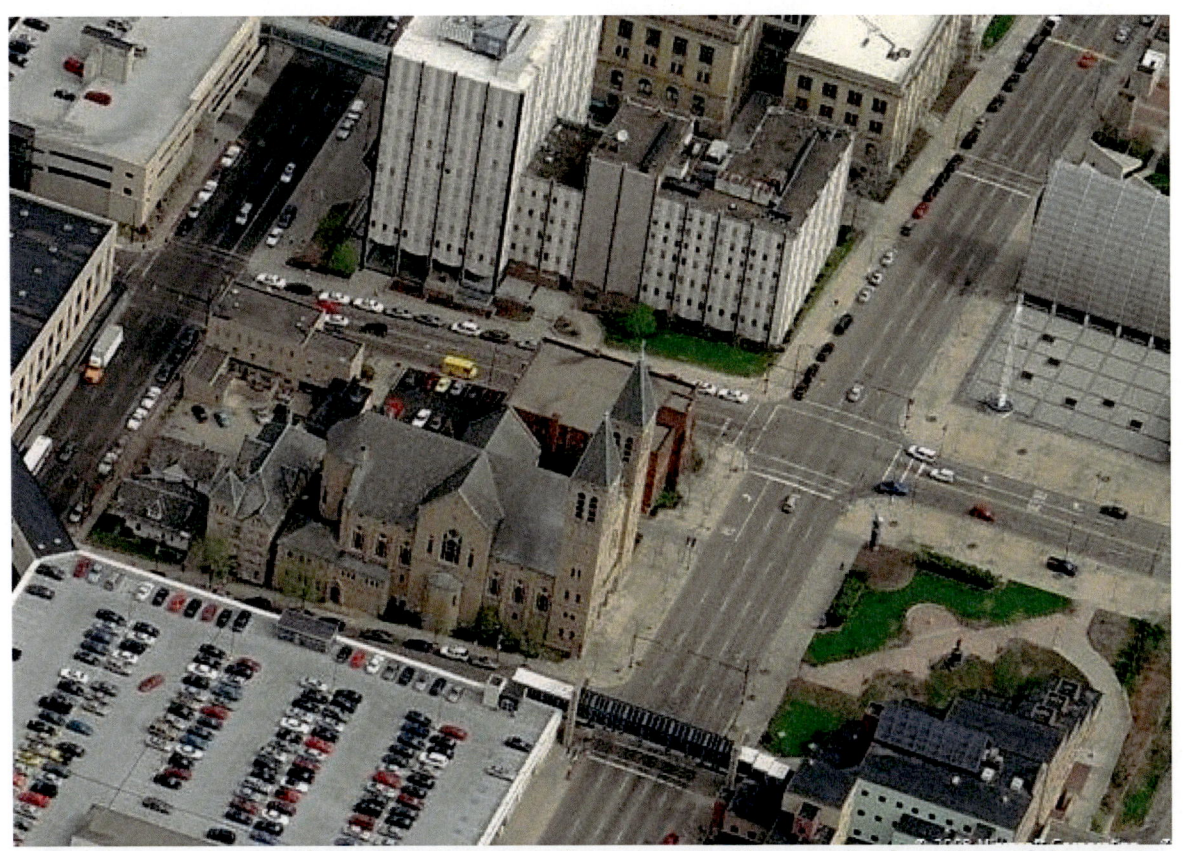

Microsoft product screen shot reprinted with permission from Microsoft Corporation.

Used with the permission of St Bernard Church.

St. Bernard, Akron, Roman Catholic

Used with the permission of St Bernard Church.

Used with the permission of St Bernard Church.

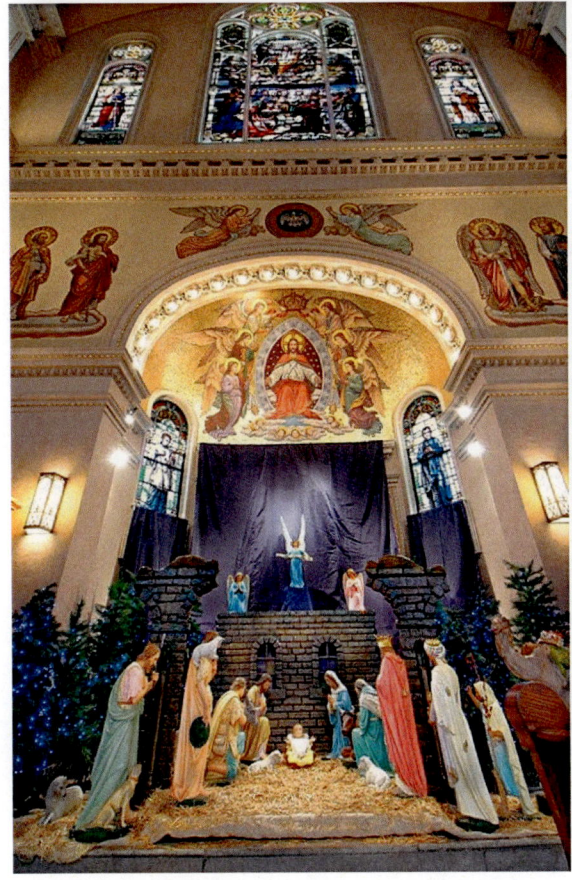

St. Bernard, Akron, Roman Catholic

Ss. Cosmas and Damian, Twinsburg, Roman Catholic

Established in 1963. This parish in Twinsburg was named because Saints Cosmas and Damian were twins.

Ss. Cyril and Methodius, Barberton, Slovak, Roman Catholic

Microsoft product screen shot reprinted with permission from Microsoft Corporation.

Ss. Cyril and Methodius, Barberton, Slovak, Roman Catholic

Ss. Cyril and Methodius, Barberton, Slovak, Roman Catholic

Established in 1905. The church was completed in 1931. The parish was closed in 2009.

The window from Ss. Cyril and Methodius below is preserved in the Museum of Divine Images in Lakewood, Ohio. The museum's statue of St. Sebastian (foreground), from St. George Church in Cleveland, is identical to the one that was in the War Memorial in the original St. Sebastian Church in West Akron. The monument no longer exists.

St. Demetrius, Fairlawn, Serbian Orthodox

Established in 1919. The first church was built in 1929 on Lake Street in Akron. The present church was built in Fairlawn in 1995.

Old church on Lake Street.

St. Demetrius, Fairlawn, Serbian Orthodox

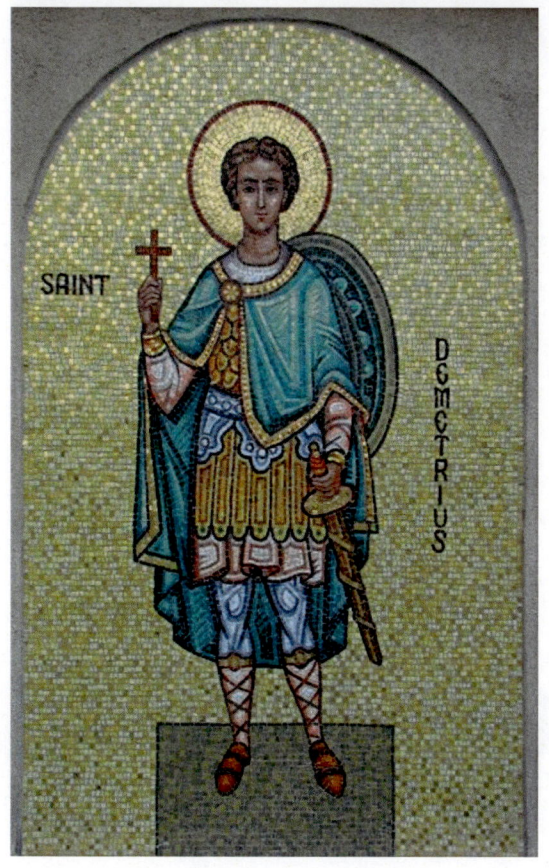

St. Edward Chapel, Fairlawn, Roman Catholic

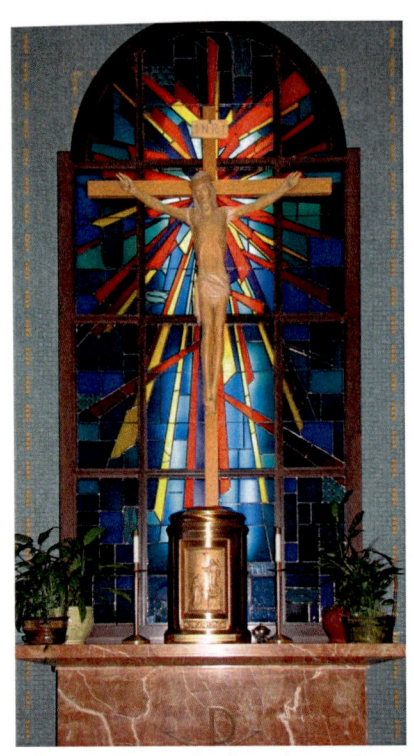

The chapel serves the Village of St. Edward and was dedicated on June 27, 1964.

St. Edward Chapel, Fairlawn, Roman Catholic

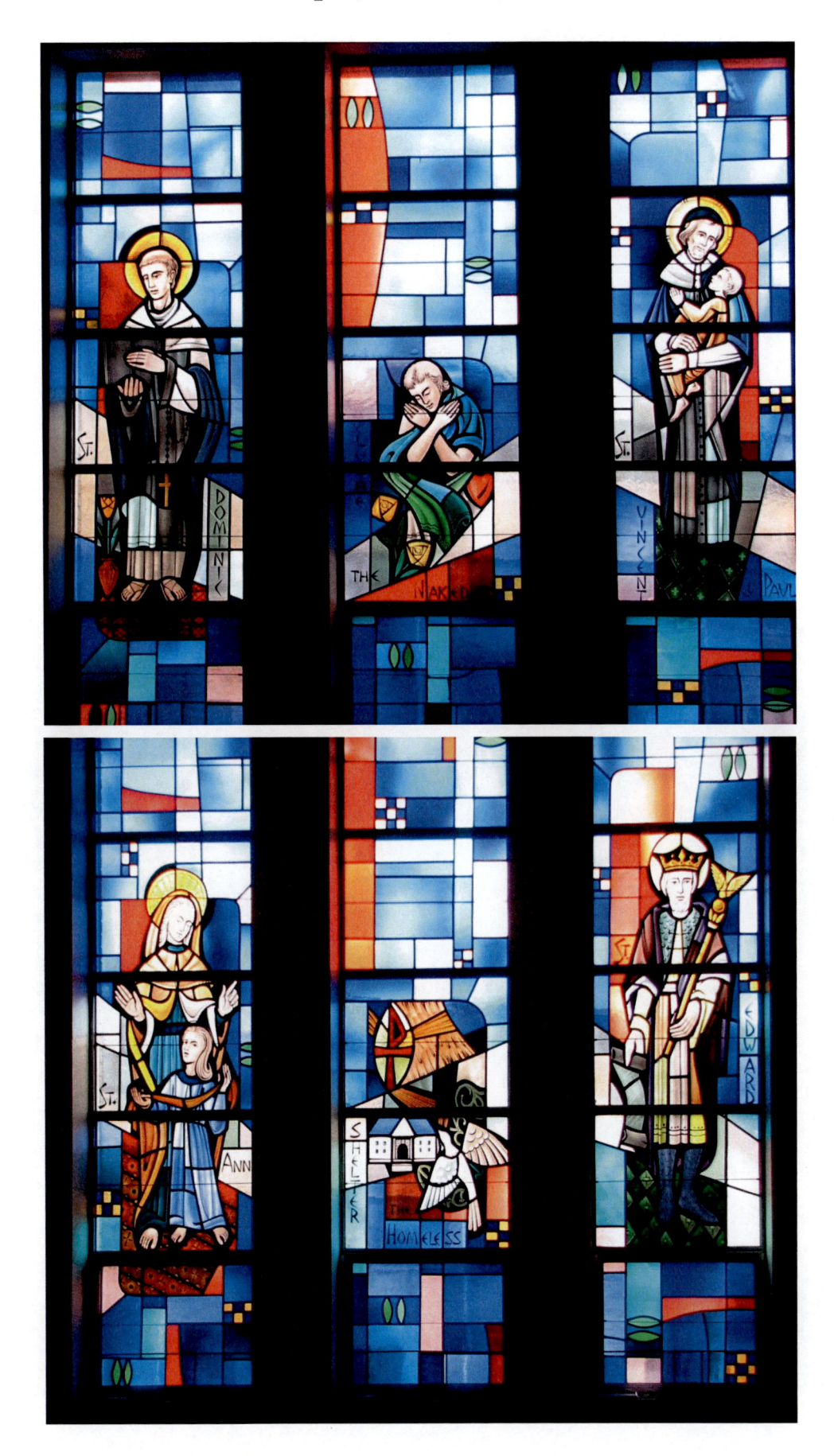

St. Elia the Prophet, Akron, Macedonian-Bulgarian Orthodox

Built in 1938.

St. Eugene, Cuyahoga Falls, Roman Catholic

Established in 1963.

St. Francis de Sales, Akron (Coventry Twp), Roman Catholic

Microsoft product screen shot reprinted with permission from Microsoft Corporation.

St. Francis de Sales, Akron (Coventry Twp), Roman Catholic

The first church, on the top floor of the school, was dedicated on May 20, 1951; the second church, now the school's gymnasium, was opened in 1955; the present church was built in 1971 at the cost of $525,000.

St. George, Clinton, Roman Catholic

St. George, Clinton, Roman Catholic

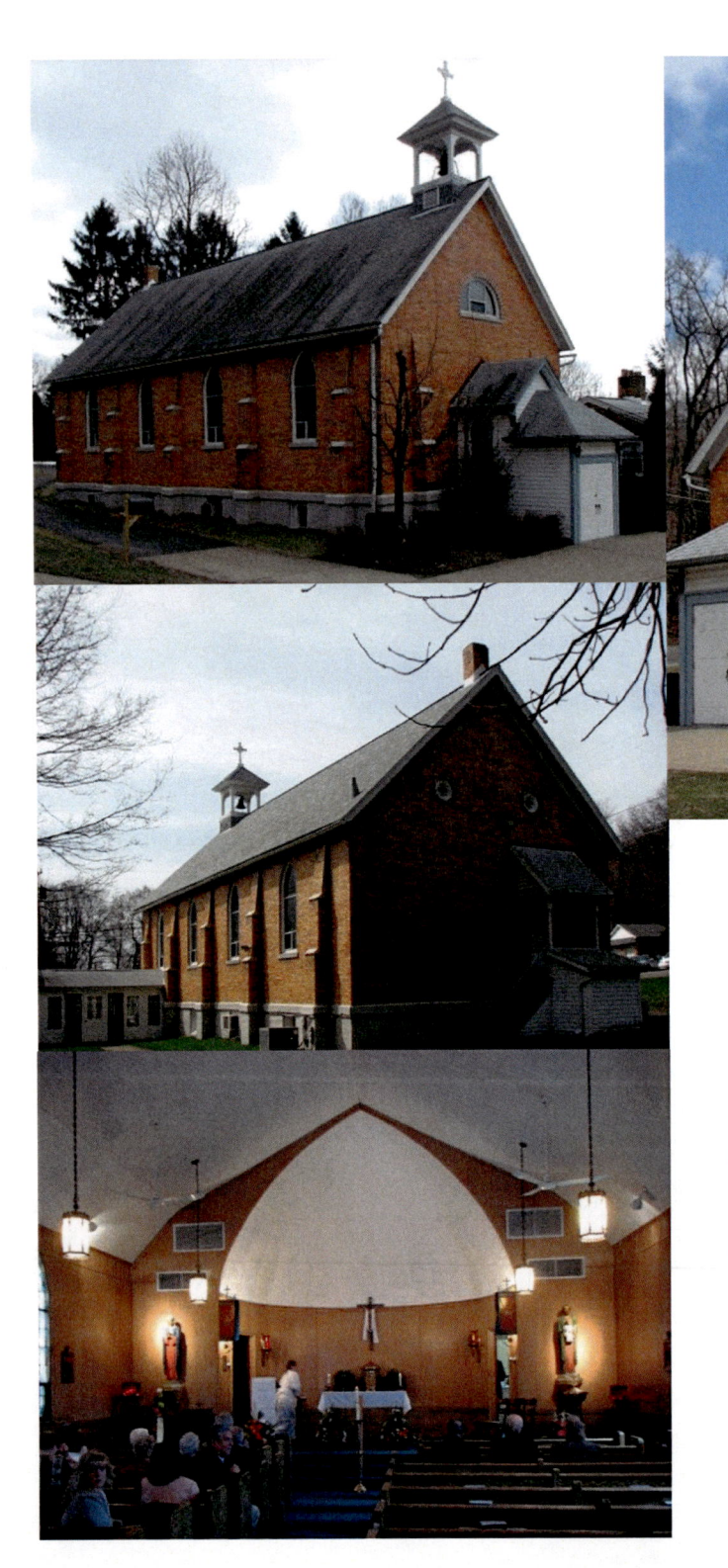

Established in 1905. The church was completed in 1908; the parish closed in 2008.

St. George, Fairlawn, Antiochean Orthodox

Established about 1915. The first church was built in Akron at the corner of Water and Cedar Streets, the present in Fairlawn in 1987.

St. Hedwig, Akron, Polish, Roman Catholic

Established in 1912. A frame church was built on Flowers Court in the Little Cuyahoga valley; it was demolished when the viaduct to North Hill was built. The brick church and school on Glenwood Avenue were dedicated on December 25, 1925. The parish was closed in 2009.

St. Hilary, Fairlawn, Roman Catholic

Established in 1958. The present building was dedicated December 4, 1966; it was extensively renovated in 1987, when the pipe organ was installed.

Microsoft product screen shot reprinted with permission from Microsoft Corporation.

St. Hilary, Fairlawn, Roman Catholic

80

St. Hilary, Fairlawn, Roman Catholic

St. John the Baptist, Akron, Slovak, Roman Catholic

Established in 1907. The Slovaks and Polish bought the old St. Bernard Church in 1908. The parish school was built on Clay Drive in 1928, and the church was dedicated there on December 21, 1941.

St. Joseph, Akron, Melchite Catholic

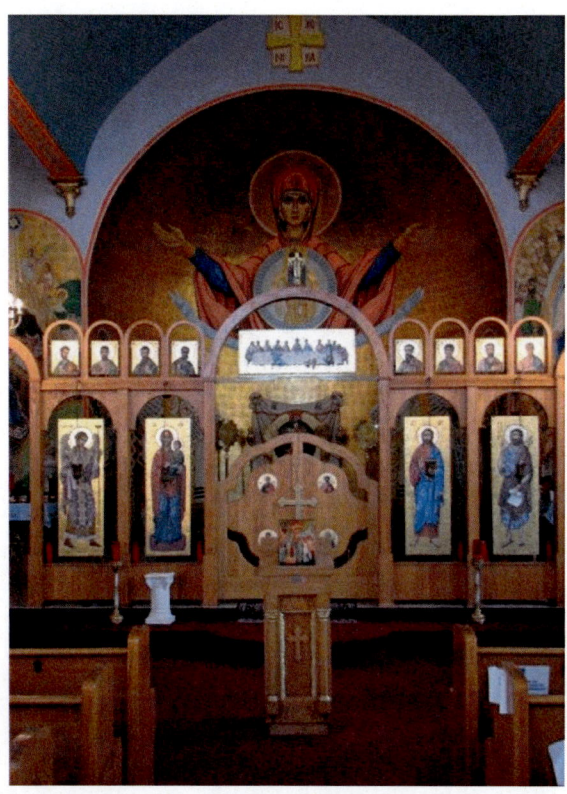

Established in 1915. The original church on Locust Street was destroyed in the 1943 tornado (below). The present brick church on West Exchange Street was dedicated on May 22, 1948.

St. Joseph, Cuyahoga Falls, Roman Catholic

Established in 1831. It was a station, then a mission, and became a parish in 1904. The present brick church was built in 1912 and enlarged in 1933.

St. Joseph, Cuyahoga Falls, Roman Catholic

St. Joseph, Randolph Twp, Roman Catholic

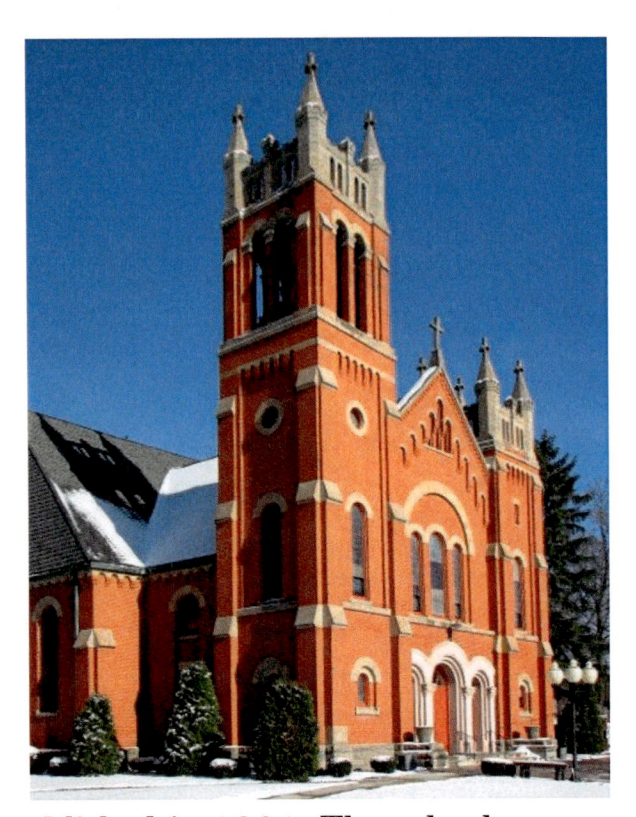

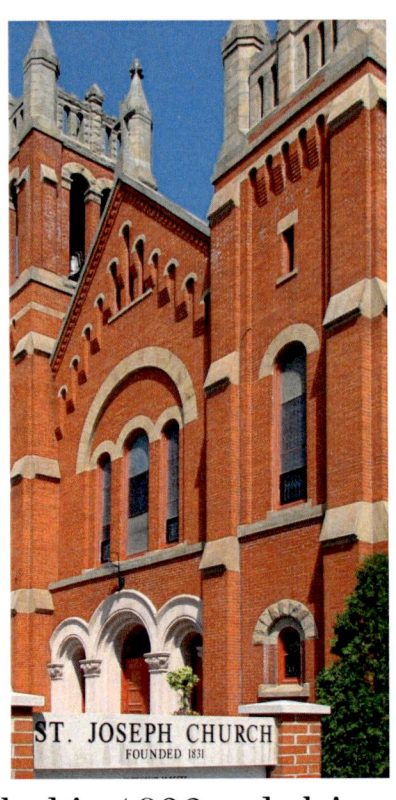

Established in 1831. The school was established in 1832 and claims to be the oldest parish school west of the Alleghenies. In 1841, St. John Neumann served as parish priest. A wooden church was built in 1864 at the cost of $15,000; this church burned down on April 21, 1904. The present brick church was dedicated on June 26, 1905. Behind the church, an old stone quarry was turned into a Lourdes Grotto and dedicated on August 14, 1927.

St. Joseph, Randolph Twp, Roman Catholic

The old wooden church, burned in 1904.

Microsoft product screen shot reprinted with permission from Microsoft Corporation.

St. Joseph, Randolph Twp, Roman Catholic

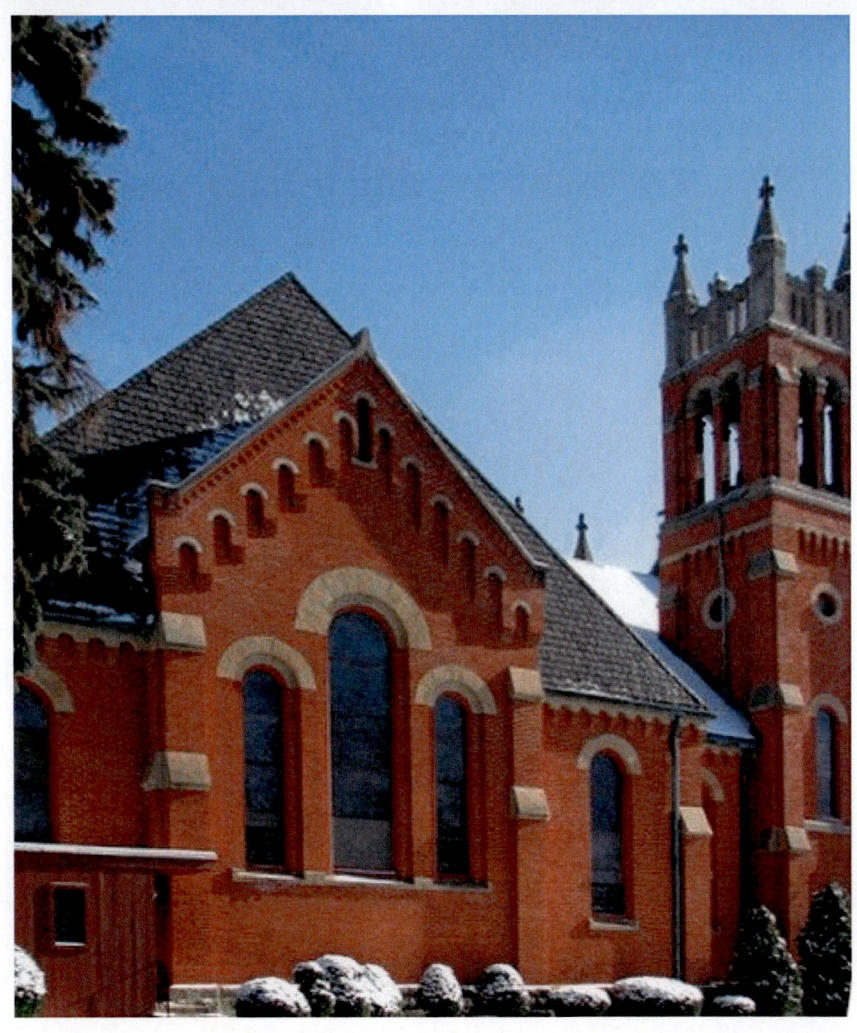

St. Joseph, Randolph Twp, Roman Catholic

St. Martha, Akron, Roman Catholic

St. Martha, Akron, Roman Catholic

Established on North Hill in 1919. In 2009, it was merged with Christ the King Parish to become Blessed Trinity Parish.

St. Mary, Akron, Roman Catholic

Established in 1887. The present basilica-style stone church was dedicated on October 1, 1916; it cost $120,000.

Microsoft product screen shot reprinted with permission from Microsoft Corporation.

St. Mary, Akron, Roman Catholic

Monday, August 3, 1964

Town Crier
A 'Basilica' In Akron

By KENNETH NICHOLS

THE SIGHTS and sounds of Akron: If you're pressed for time — or cash — it isn't necessary to go to Europe to view ancient buildings.

We have in our town a structure that is at least 1,641 years old — by design.

It is an anachronism, in a sense, since the building is set down in the heart of a city that — as a city — is yet to celebrate its 100th birthday.

This church of St. Mary on Coburn st. at Thornton st. actually is — by design — older than Christianity because the basic plan harkens back to the pagan days of Rome.

St. Mary is an oblong basilica, the type constructed by Roman emperors as public meeting places and law courts. The term, "basilica," was used by them in the sense of "hall" (in the original Greek it meant "royal").

★

OVER THE centuries, after the Christian church emerged from the catacombs, the oblong basilica plan with evolving stylistic variants became the standard for churches of Western Christendom.

But St. Mary is not just "a" basilica.

St. Mary is a reproduction of the Duomo, the cathedral church of Ostia, the town at the mouth of the Tiber in Italy, 14 miles from Rome and — by legend — the first colony founded by Rome.

The Duomo was altered over the centuries — especially the facade or front side — but those alterations faithfully appear in reproduction at the church on Coburn st.

★

THERE IS another fact about St. Mary which should interest anyone desiring to take the quick and inexpensive tour to Rome and the beginning centuries of Christianity.

The Duomo and its twin are similar in general outline to Old St. Peter's basilica at Rome, so called because it was razed in the 16th century to make way for the present St. Peter's.

At St. Mary, the apse and the transept — those additions that gave the basilica the shape of a Latin cross — are rounded, just like the Duomo's. Those of Old St. Peter were angular. There's the only great difference.

And construction started on Old St. Peter's in 323 A. D. It was dedicated in 326 A. D.

★

OLD ST. PETER had at its front door an "atrium," an open courtyard that provided facilities for the instruction of converts and offices for church officials.

St. Mary has no atrium but it has above the main doorway a window that reflects yet another development of church architecture over the span of time. It is a rosette window, a borrowing from the great Gothic cathedrals constructed during the 12th and 13th centuries in Europe, largely France.

On the Thornton st. side of the church is another variant that came down from medieval times. This is the "campanile" or bell tower.

★

HOW OLD is St. Mary by construction? Plans to build it were formulated by then Father Joseph S. O'Keefe a few months after he arrived here as the new pastor in 1914. Akron had an estimated population then of 98,000.

The church — constructed at a cost of $120,000 — was dedicated on Oct. 1, 1916. And the sermon was preached by Father Edward A. Mooney, later Cardinal Mooney, Archbishop of Detroit.

An American "tourist" in South Akron will find another way in which St. Mary follows the tradition established by the first basilicas. It is oriented so that the congregation faces the rising sun... to commemorate the Eastertide resurrection of Christ.

ST. MARY CHURCH IN AKRON

OLD ST. PETER BASILICA IN ROME

Reprinted with permission from the Akron Beacon Journal and Ohio.com.

When Old St. Mary Was Chapel Of Ease

By KENNETH NICHOLS

MARY'S CHURCH: The Star Hotel at 658 S. Main st. is not an imposing place although the property includes three buildings.

A motorist, pressed hard by traffic in the narrow street, would pass the hostelry without a second glance and, so, never know that it is clean, well-kept, well-managed.

The outward appearance of the brick and imitation brick-sided buildings belie their importance to the Akron story and to the greater story of Christmas.

One of the buildings, the main two-story brick structure, was the original home of a Catholic mission established in 1887 by St. Vincent de Paul Church and called "The Chapel of Ease."

Nichols

Akron then was a city of, perhaps 20,000 — the official population count in 1880 was 16,462 — and the mission, opposite McCoy st., was only a few blocks south of the original town limits established in 1825.

See TOWN CRIER, Page 14

(Continued From Page 1)

But then came the rubber boom, first a demand for tires for buggies and bicycles and then for autos, and by the early 1890s the number of people here had almost doubled.

The time came in 1896 to make the Chapel of Ease a parish church. That was done and the church was named for the sainted Mary, the Mother of God.

★

JUST A YEAR before St. Mary parish was established, the first building — which had served as both school and chapel — had seen the construction of a near neighbor to the south.

The near neighbor was a new chapel, a long frame building with a gabled roof.

It was no accident that the roof of the chapel was gabled. A publication of St. Mary parish issued in 1947 on the occasion of its Golden Jubilee had this to say:

"In Rome, the Eternal City, there stands yet today the Baths of Caracalla — a vestige of Rome's grandeur as the Imperial City. Opposite these baths is one of the earliest of the Christian basilicas, a humble, barn-like edifice with gabled roof, erected when the Church dared first to emerge from the Catacombs."

Such was the first St. Mary church... "a humble, barn-like edifice with gabled roof."

★

IT WAS PRESUMED, we suppose, in the early years that the church of St. Mary would never have another home. At any rate, as late as 1898 a pastoral residence of brick was built next to the church and a frame house provided for the Sisters who taught the school.

The first entry found in the baptismal record was that of Thomas Hanifin, baptized Jan. 10, 1897. He was later ordained a priest.

But the people came on — in a flood after 1910 — and "South Akron," and St. Mary, became more and more "downtown" as the rows of new houses stretched block after block to "the country" around Wilbeth rd.

By 1914, the population of the town was more than 98,000 and in that year, Fr. Joseph S. O'Keefe, two months after his arrival at St. Mary as pastor, started construction of a new church at Coburn and Thornton sts.

The cornerstone of the present St. Mary was laid in 1915. It, the church building, is said to be a reproduction of the Duomo, the Cathedral Church of Ostia, outside Rome.

★

AND WHAT of the old buildings? They were purchased by a construction company owner, Thomas E. McShaffery, and some associates. In 1917 they put a new front on the onetime chapel-school and converted it into a hotel. The frame church building, in time, became a men's dormitory.

In '17, a World War I year, factory workers slept in shifts in overcrowded rooming houses. Even the shelves above stairways were used as bunks. There was no room in any inn.

So rightly it seems, that the first buildings of the church named for Mary, should then — and now — be a place where the traveller or another can find rest... a room at an inn.

St. Mary, Akron, Roman Catholic

The Summit County Historical Society of Akron, OH; housed at the Akron-Summit County Public Library.

The old wooden church, with a circus parade going by.

St. Mary, Akron, Roman Catholic

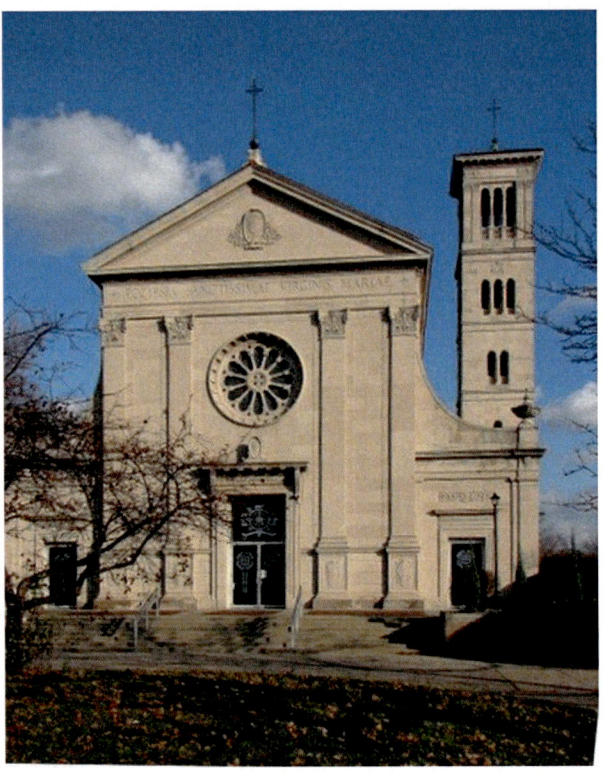

St. Mary, Akron, Orthodox

St. Mary, Hudson, Roman Catholic

Established in 1860. The original white frame church is located on the Green in central Hudson. A new church was built on north Main Street and dedicated on December 8, 1972. The present church was dedicated on June 10, 1995.

St. Mary, Hudson, Roman Catholic

St. Matthew, Akron, Roman Catholic

Microsoft product screen shot reprinted with permission from Microsoft Corporation.

Establiished in 1943. The church was built in 1955, and the first Mass was celebrated in it on February 5, 1956.

St. Michael, Akron, Byzantine Catholic

St. Michael, Akron, Byzantine Catholic

Established 1916. Now closed.

99

St. Nicholas, Barberton (Coventry Twp), Byzantine Catholic

St. Nicholas, Barberton (Coventry Twp), Byzantine Catholic

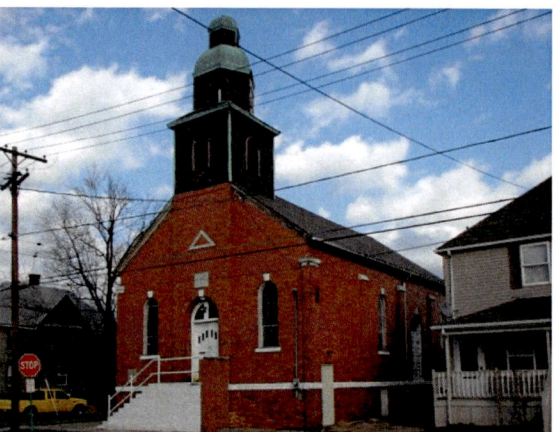

Old church, Barberton

Established in Barberton in 1916. The present round church was built in 1966.

Microsoft product screen shot reprinted with permission from Microsoft Corporation.

St. Nicholas, Mogadore (Suffield Twp), Russian Orthodox

Established in Akron in 1917. The parish moved to its present site in 1984.

St. Nicholas, Mogadore (Suffield Twp), Russian Orthodox

St. Nicholas, Mogadore (Suffield Twp), Russian Orthodox

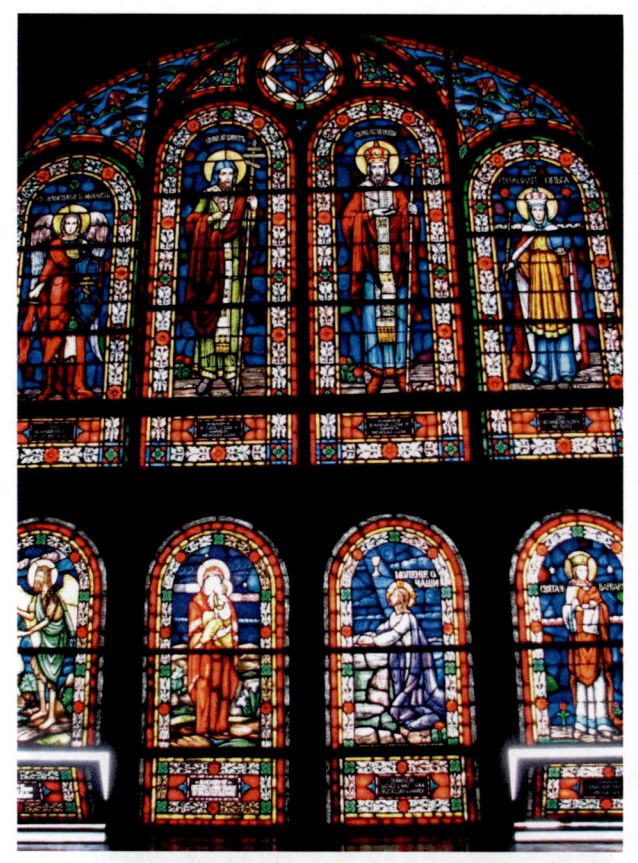

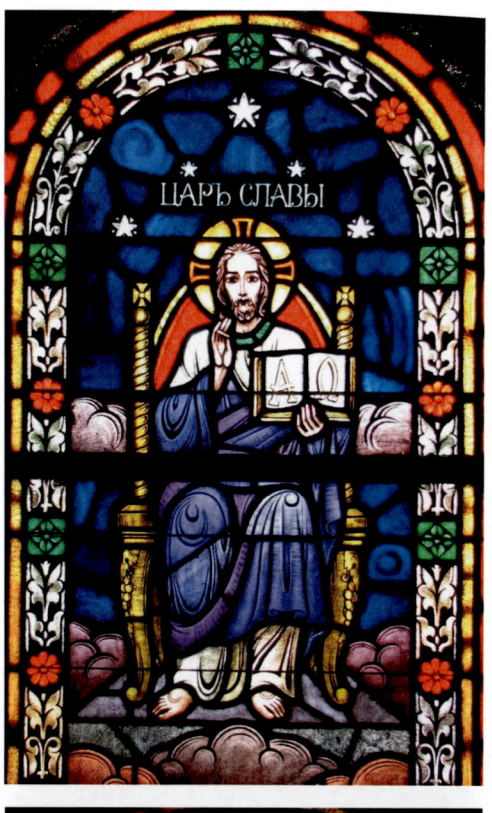

St. Nikola, Green, Macedonian Orthodox

St. Patrick, Kent, Roman Catholic

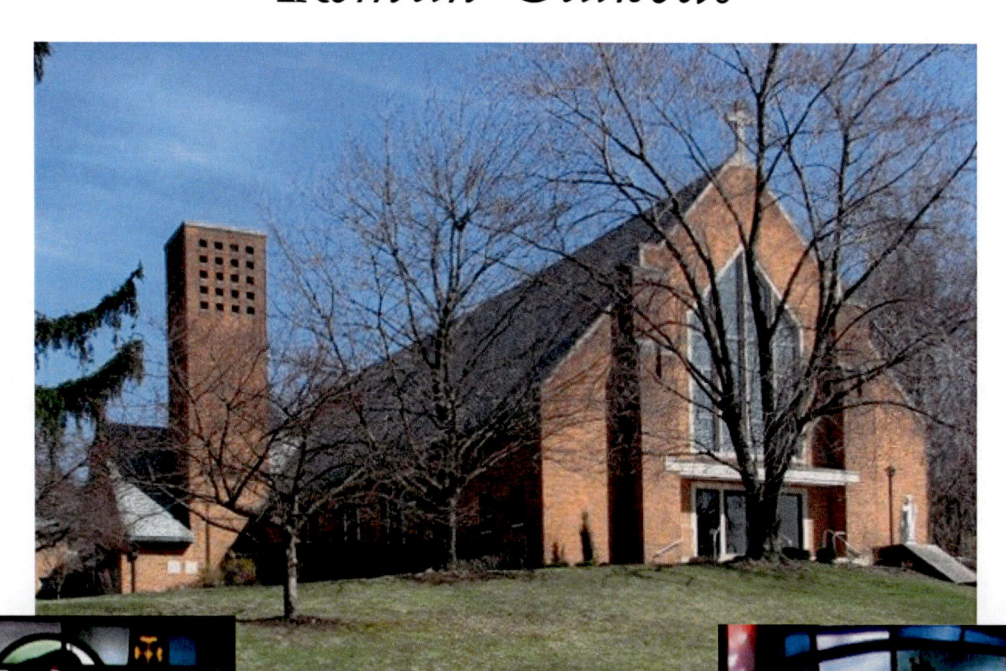

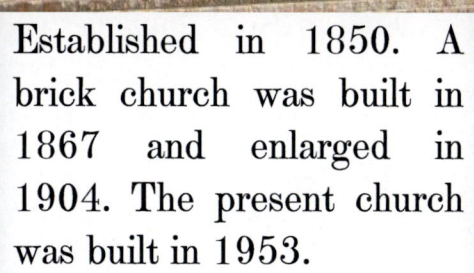

Established in 1850. A brick church was built in 1867 and enlarged in 1904. The present church was built in 1953.

Windows of the other apostles are in the church itself and can be seen from the altar. The window of Judas Iscariot (right) is at a side entrance, out of sight from the altar. It is not known whose idea it was, but this window is quite unique.

105

St. Paul, Akron (Firestone Park), Roman Catholic

Established in 1919. The present church was dedicated on October 26, 2003.

Microsoft product screen shot reprinted with permission from Microsoft Corporation.

St. Paul, Akron (Firestone Park), Roman Catholic

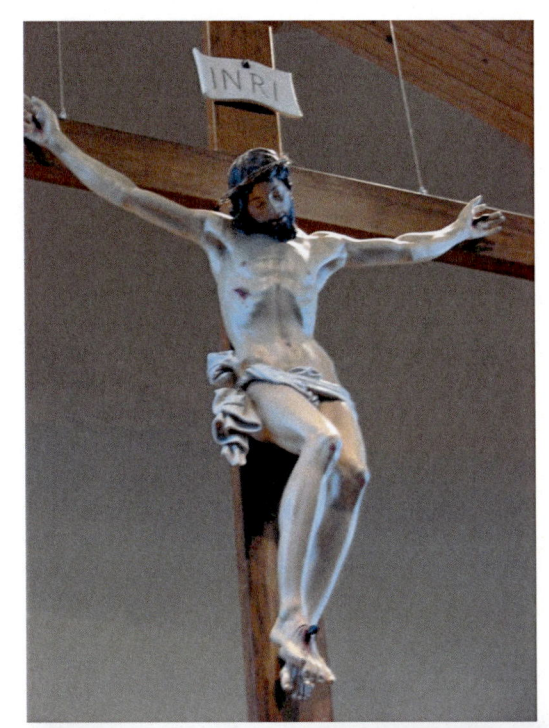

The original church is shown above and its Altar is to the right; that Altar is preserved in the new church.

107

St. Peter, Akron (Sherbondy Hill), Roman Catholic

Established in 1917 as a Lithuanian parish; in 1926, it became a territorial parish. It was closed in 1990.

The old church in Akron.

St. Peter Claver, Akron, Roman Catholic

Established in 1945 as a parish for black Catholics. No pictures can be found.

St. Peter Claver Church, Akron

By September 1945, Monsignor O'Keefe found suitable property which had 3 houses and a brick building with living quarters above for $18,000 on W. Bartges St. St. Peter Claver parish was canonically erected in November 1945 to serve the African American Catholic community in all of Summit County.

A Precious Blood priest, Father Anthony Kraff, said the first Mass on Dec. 23, 1945 and served as the first pastor until October 1946 when due to difficulties between himself and a large group of parishioners, Bishop Hoban appointed Father Vincent Haas to serve as pastor. Father Haas had worked with the Third Order as well as some of the people. The two goals of the parish were "to teach the Negroes of Akron the Faith and to build a better understanding between the colored and whites in Akron." To these ends, Father Haas continued the St. Peter Claver Interracial Forum as well as establishing a Holy Name Society, an Alcoholics Anonymous group, a CYO for teens, and a sewing group. When Father Haas was appointed full time chaplain at St. Thomas Hospital in 1948, he moved to the hospital but continued to offer Sunday Mass at the parish as well as other services.

However, because the parish, established just for African American Catholics in order to provide them with a stable place to worship, covered all of Summit County, many potential parishioners worshiped at their neighborhood churches and were involved with the Catholic schools their children often attended.

By 1952, Father Haas noted that "the graceful acceptance into other parishes" of the potential parishioners as well as his other full time duties contrived to make St. Peter Claver to be similar to mission status. Haas himself believed that the "Negroes should find worship and development of their Faith within their own parish boundaries" even while acknowledging that probably a priest needed to be appointed in those parishes to be a liaison between the white and black parishioners.

By 1958 when Father Haas was transferred, the total Catholic population of St. Peter Claver was listed as 47. Father Adelbert Gassert was appointed chaplain at St. Thomas and final pastor of St. Peter. The property was sold in 1959 and the last Mass said there July 19, 1959. The records were turned over to St. Mary's and the church furnishings sent to the newly created St. Albert the Great church, North Royalton.

St. Peter of the Fields, Rootstown, Roman Catholic

St. Peter of the Fields, Rootstown, Roman Catholic

Established 1868; the cemetery dates back to the 1830s. The old church is preserved, and the new chuch was dedicated on November 26, 2006.

Ss. Peter and Paul, Doylestown, Roman Catholic

Established in 1827. The school was established in 1862. The present brick church was dedicated on October 22, 1880.

Ss. Philip and James, Canal Fulton, Roman Catholic

Established in 1845. The school was established in 1866. The brick church was dedicated in 1869 and cost $28,000.

St. Sebastian, Akron, Roman Catholic

St. Sebastian, Akron, Roman Catholic

Microsoft product screen shot reprinted with permission from Microsoft Corporation.

St. Sebastian, Akron, Roman Catholic

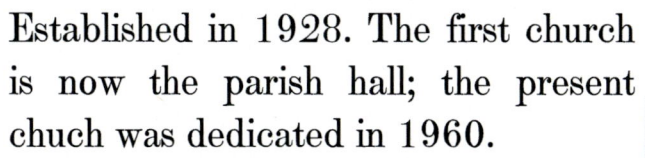

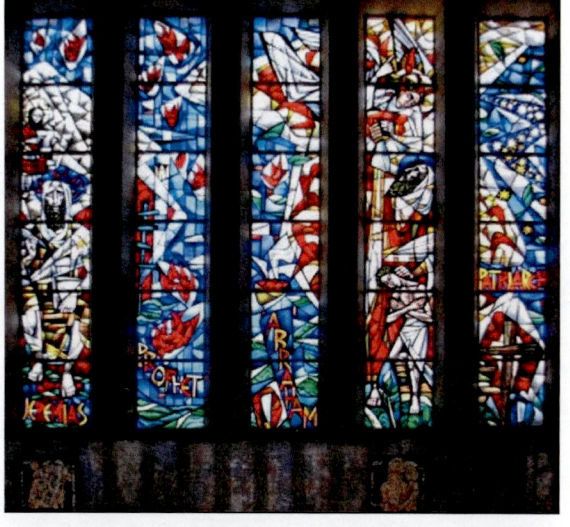

Established in 1928. The first church is now the parish hall; the present chuch was dedicated in 1960.

115

St. Thomas Hospital Chapel, Akron

DR. BOB'S WAY

Dr. Robert H. Smith, an Akron physician, fondly remembered as "Dr. Bob," worked with Sister Mary Ignatia and St. Thomas Hospital to acknowledge alcoholism as a medical condition. The first alcoholic patient was admitted with dignity through the front doors of St. Thomas Hospital on August 16, 1939. The work of Sister Ignatia and Dr. Bob is remembered by countless members of Alcoholics Anonymous. This roadway represents a heritage of courage and hope for alcoholics and their families.

It is with pride and gratitude that the Summa Foundation commemorates the important role of St. Thomas Hospital, Sister Ignatia and Dr. Bob in the treatment of alcoholism.

St. Thomas Hospital Chapel, Akron

The chapel was opened in 1938; it was staffed by the Sisters of Charity of St. Augustine. From a sign in the chapel: "In this chapel and the adjacent hospital ward, thousands of alcoholics from across the country found sobriety. It was with the spiritual guidance of Sister Mary Ignatia, the medical and moral support of Alcoholics Anonymous cofounder Dr. Bob Smith, and the help of fellow recovering alcoholics that the first AA ward found success.

"With the help of many in the medical, religious and AA communities, this exhibit focuses on the story of Sister Mary Ignatia and the central role she played in establishing the first AA ward. It includes the story of Alcoholics Anonymous and its cofounders, Dr. Bob Smith and Bill Wilson. This center also pays tribute to the Sisters of Charity, whose care and spiritual guidance for revering alcoholics never waned."

St. Thomas, Fairlawn, Bulgarian Orthodox

Established in 1960. The present church was built in 1978.

St. Victor, Richfield, Roman Catholic

Established in 1964; the church was dedicated on November 6, 1966.

St. Vincent de Paul, Akron, Roman Catholic

Established in 1837. A frame church was built in 1844 on Green Street (where the high school football stadium is now); a school was established in 1853. With stone quarried in Peninsula, the present stone church was built during the Civil War and was dedicated on March 17, 1866 at the cost of $50,000. The rectory was built in 1884.

St. Vincent de Paul, Akron, Roman Catholic

The Summit County Historical Society of Akron, OH; housed at Akron-Summit County Public Library.

St. Vincent in 1874, at the top of the hill on the left.

Microsoft product screen shot reprinted with permission from Microsoft Corporation.

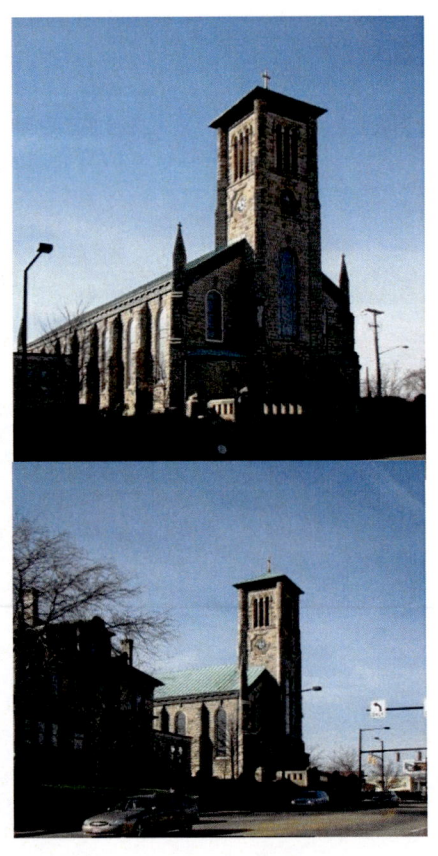

120

St. Vincent de Paul, Akron, Roman Catholic

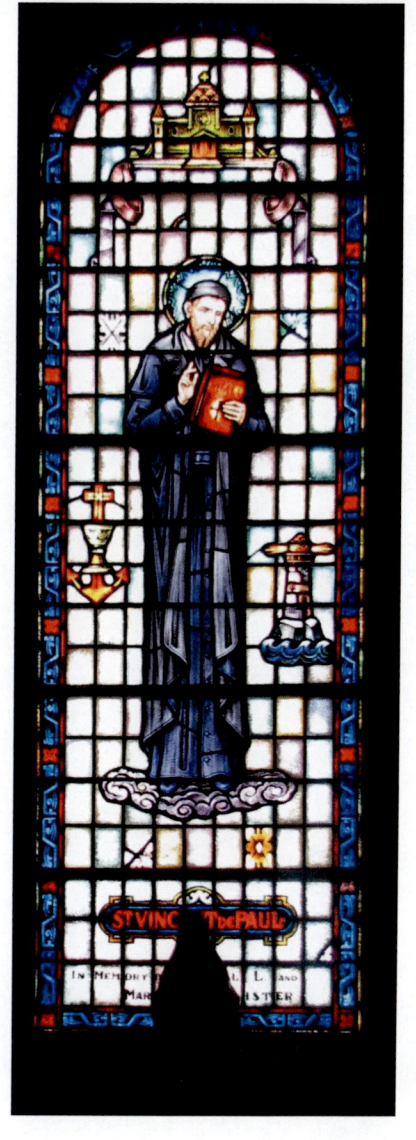

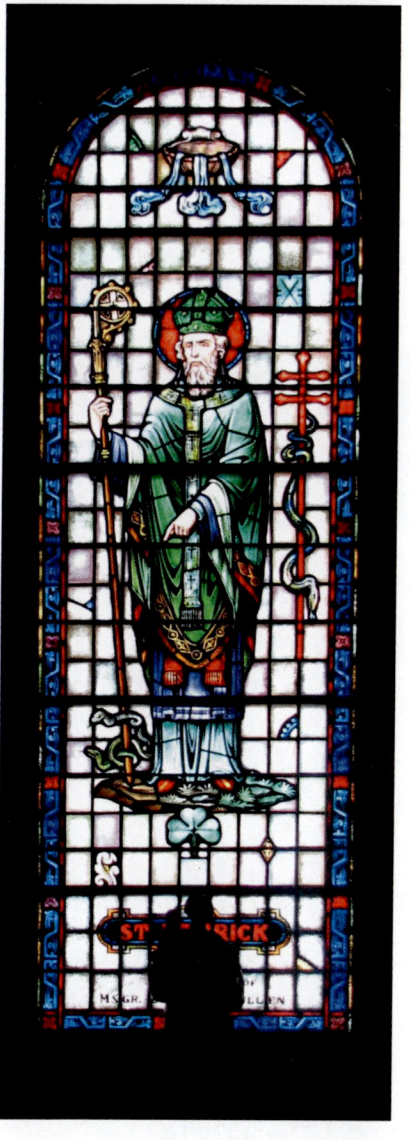

121

Made in the USA
Middletown, DE
13 February 2015